# You Are the Storm
## Event Reflections

"Thank you just doesn't seem like enough! But all
I can say is I thank God for using you as a mighty
vessel. The hand of God was all over that place!
I was set free and released and rejuvenated in a
way like [sic] I haven't been in a while!
It was so warm, fun, and welcoming!
I am still in awe of the movement!"

**- Lisa S.**

"It was such a great event. Thanks for being you
and pouring into others!"

**- Lillian T.**

# You ARE THE STORM

## A JOURNAL OF MY JOURNEY TO YOU

# You ARE THE STORM

## A JOURNAL OF MY JOURNEY TO YOU

STEPHANIE R. PARHAM

Halo
PUBLISHING
INTERNATIONAL

Halo Publishing International
7550 WIH-10 #800, PMB 2069,
San Antonio, TX 78229

First Edition, October 2023
ISBN: 978-1-63765-524-5
Library of Congress Control Number: 2023907447

The information contained within this book is strictly for informational purposes. Unless otherwise indicated, all the names, characters, businesses, places, events and incidents in this book are either the product of the author's imagination or used in a fictitious manner. Any resemblance to actual persons, living or dead, or actual events is purely coincidental.

Halo Publishing International is a self-publishing company that publishes adult fiction and non-fiction, children's literature, self-help, spiritual, and faith-based books. We continually strive to help authors reach their publishing goals and provide many different services that help them do so. We do not publish books that are deemed to be politically, religiously, or socially disrespectful, or books that are sexually provocative, including erotica. Halo reserves the right to refuse publication of any manuscript if it is deemed not to be in line with our principles. Do you have a book idea you would like us to consider publishing? Please visit www.halopublishing.com for more information.

I dedicate this book to my mother, Carolyn Waddy. Mom, thank you for being my first teacher by laying the foundation for motherhood, education, and love for God. Your sacrifices created opportunities, and your example established a standard.

Love,
Steph

# Contents

# Introduction

You Are the Storm, a dramatic ministry event, was envisioned prior to the global pandemic of 2020. In September of the previous year, I heard the Holy Spirit say:

*There is a necessity in the earth*
*for young women to understand*
*their worth and power.*

However, I only received glimpses of the actual details of this upcoming event. Yet I understood that there would be a gathering of women who needed to hear a message from God. In November of 2022, I saw more detailed visions of how the event would transpire, and the Holy Spirit spoke very clearly:

*It must happen at the top of the*
*year, because it sets the tone for*
*the rest of the year!*

You Are the Storm was staffed, designed, and conducted within two months!

Yet in the midst of extraordinary planning and collaboration, I was further instructed to write this journal that would connect us. God wanted you to see that my strengths, weaknesses, obedience, and disobedience would not usurp His masterful plan for YOU!

*And blessed is she who believed*
*that there would be a fulfillment*
*of what had been spoken to*
*her by the Lord.*

(Luke 1:45, New American
Standard Bible 2020)

# Day 1

I cried as I heard God tell me to begin this journal in preparation for you. I knew that this under-taking would require a great sacrifice, and the spirit of **fear** was beginning to reach for me. You see, there is nothing about this upcoming event that is entertaining or easy. It requires an undying commitment to do exactly what God has asked me to do. That alone scares me!

Trusting Him was the only way to produce an experience that would change the lives of the women that He'd called to a specific place. My prayer is that you receive what God intended for you. You are his beautiful creation, and if your feet landed in this space today, it means that some-where, somehow, you've forgotten that…

## YOU ARE THE STORM!

*For God has not given us a*
*spirit of timidity, but of power*
*and love and discipline.*

(2 Timothy 1:7)

# Today's Focus: Fear

Define **fear.**

Describe what you feel when you're **afraid.**
(Physical symptoms?)

# Today's Focus: Fear

List one **fear** that you're currently facing.

List one step that you can take to overcome that **fear**.

# Day 2

Today's message was actually inspired by the events of last night. As I prepared an unhealthy snack and beverage, the Holy Spirit informed me that I would be drinking water for the remainder of this time of preparation. Although I understood His reasoning, I didn't want to admit how much I struggle with sugar. It was then that God began to show me that part of this journey was embracing specific **addictions** that cause all of us to struggle.

Frequently, we measure our various food addictions by how much they impact our size. Yet the reality is addictions impact us differently. As a woman who's overcome years of pain, oppression, depression, and fear, sugar became my vice. Unfortunately, the end result was extensive dental treatment, pain, and embarrassment. While it may sound minimal to someone who struggles with other kinds of addictions, there is a silent pain that accompanies all struggles.

Be encouraged! As I embark upon this new direction from God, I'm praying for your release from addiction. We are God's vessels that were created to bring Him honor. Otherwise, the addiction becomes a stronghold over our lives, one that feels impossible to overcome.

> *No weapon that is formed*
> *against you will succeed…*

(Isaiah 54:17)

# Today's Focus: Addiction

## What is **addiction**?

## What feelings/behaviors tell you that you have an **addiction**?

# Today's Focus: Addiction

Explain how **addiction** has affected your journey.

What step(s) can you take to overcome the **addiction**?

# Day 3

Today was filled with the following opportunities:

1. An entrepreneurial networking event
2. My cousin's speaking engagement
3. My friend's church event

Yet, **obeying** God's voice had to be the determining factor in my decision-making. By honoring my commitment to support my cousin's speaking engagement, I had the opportunity to discover that she had stepped into entrepreneurship and developed her own company. I witnessed an amazing presentation that revealed what I never would have known about her!

The second act of obedience involved the purchase of a money order (no kidding). While preparing to purchase a money order from a local grocery store, I clearly felt led to go to Walmart. However, it was more convenient to go to the grocery store closer to my house. When I arrived at this store, there was an extremely long line. This time, when I heard the Holy Spirit say, "Go to Walmart," I obeyed.

While waiting in line at Walmart, I saw a woman walking with a cane and pushing a cart. I asked her how she was doing, and she said, "I'm having a difficult time because I had knee replacement surgery." I asked if the surgery was recent, and she said, "It was six months ago."

I heard the Holy Spirit say, "Pray for her," so I asked her for permission to pray, and she agreed. The power of God was present as we joined hands and began to pray. After prayer, we embraced because it was clear to both of us that God had met us in the store.

However, when I got back in line to purchase the money order, the sales clerk said, "The money order machine is not working." My newfound sister in faith and I looked at each other and began to rejoice. It was clear that God had directed me to the store on her behalf!

Sister, this is the same Holy Spirit who is leading me directly to this event on your behalf. To God be the glory for whatever He wants to do for you!

*For where two or three have*
*gathered together in My name,*
*I am there in their midst.*

(Matthew 18:20)

# Today's Focus: Obedience

How would you define **obedience**?

How do you know when there's something
(voice/feeling) that you need to **obey**?

# Today's Focus: Obedience

Describe a time when you were **obedient**.
Describe a time when you were **disobedient**.
What was the outcome of each scenario?

What is the next instruction that you need to **obey**?

# Day 4

Today, I speak specifically to the woman who is simply **different**. You're different because you stand out in a crowd. Yet your internal desire is to somehow blend into the world of normalcy. The activity of your brain alone requires you to hyperfocus during conversations, ask for clarification, utilize active-listening strategies, and pray that you somehow remain in sync with what others say to you. Sometimes it's easier to be alone in order to avoid the eyes of judgment.

Sister, if you find yourself forced into a similar world, I understand you completely. In fact, I AM YOU! Today, God allowed me to find myself immersed in a social situation that made me feel both uncomfortable and guarded.

My daily walk with ADHD creates a world that is difficult to navigate and share with others. So I casually mention my diagnosis to some, hoping that there might be some measure of understanding during conversations. Normally, I'm met with a sarcastic remark, an eerie silence, or a dismissing comment that reminds me that my world (ADHD) is oftentimes mocked and used as an excuse for specific behaviors.

In reality, some of us just want others to understand our differences without being deemed weird.

*Do not judge, so that you*
*will not be judged.*

(Matthew 7:1)

# Today's Focus: Different

Define **different**.

What makes you feel **different**?
(Examples: appearance, thoughts, emotions, diagnoses)

# Today's Focus: Different

Describe how you handle your **difference**.

How can you use your **difference** on your journey?

# Day 5

Spiritually, today marked another level of preparation because I saw your face and your storm. As I closed my eyes to pray, I saw pain, sadness, loss, fear, and more on the faces of women like you.

As I began to walk through the specific details of what God wanted you to experience, I shared this experience with another woman of faith. She couldn't believe the details that God had given me. Interestingly, God was so specific about every detail that even while I was writing this message to you, there was a song playing on my phone about His **intentionality**. He left no stone unturned as He began to prepare me to speak to you.

*Intentional* simply means that God is allowing something to happen on purpose. He meant for certain women to show up at the event. He allowed distractions to attempt to keep you from arriving at the doorstep. He even allowed people to try to discourage you from attending by creating excuses. But God insured that you would be present.

Embrace YOUR newness. Embrace the new YOU. Embrace the power that He has given YOU! You belong to Him, and He is your God!

As you continue to read, there will be small things that will seem to be coincidental. Today's message is to reassure you that everything that appears to be coincidental is actually intentional! God had you in mind when He created this event and this journal.

> *"For I know the plans I have*
> *for you," declares the Lord,*
> *"plans for prosperity and not*
> *for disaster, to give you a*
> *future and a hope."*

(Jeremiah 29:11)

# Today's Focus: Intentional

Define **intentional**.

How do you feel about God being **intentional** in your life?

# Today's Focus: Intentional

What messages in this journal
were **intentionally** for you?

How can you use God's **intentionality**
to help you along your journey?

# Day 6

Today, I was saturated with God's presence as I assisted my brother with a painting job. You see, he always **worships** when he paints because it's his way of honoring God for his painting business. So it easily created an environment for God to speak to me and reveal more about this wonderful event. As we painted and worshipped, God brought revelations in many areas! The most significant discovery was the music that He wanted you to hear on that day. Specific songs resonated in my spirit and were clearly identified as key elements of this day's events.

God is so strategic that He handpicked the songs that would be played. As I listened to my brother's random playlist, I could sense in my spirit which songs belonged. It was so exciting that I had to focus in order to finish painting!

As God continued to move, He stirred my brother's spirit. As a result, Joe asked me thought-provoking questions that were unique to the event. It was evident that God intended for us to paint together, worship together, and continue to visualize how this experience would unfold.

Every detail of this day was important to God because you are important to Him!

*Lord, you are my God; I will*
*exalt You; I will give thanks to*
*Your name; for You have worked*
*wonders, plans formed long ago,*
*with perfect faithfulness.*

(Isaiah 25:1)

# Today's Focus: Worship

## What does **worship** mean to you?

## How does **worship** make you feel?

# Today's Focus: Worship

How might **worship** help you today?

As you continue your journey,
how could you explore **worship**?

# Day 7

Today, I'm speaking to the sister who is completely **overwhelmed**. You are fully capable of accomplishing numerous tasks within a day's time. However, the taxing nature of this type of activity only wreaks havoc on your mind, body, and soul. Therefore, God is asking both you and me to establish realistic goals for each day, without overwhelming ourselves.

One of the ways to refrain from overwhelming ourselves is to develop the ability to say no. A wise friend once told me that my yes really had no value because I rarely said no. (Ouch!) I speak the same words to you, sister. Believe me when I say, overextending myself tells me that I'm losing my balance. Frequently, it's the result of mismanaging my time. I have to learn to establish, and then maintain, a healthy balance of my responsibilities. Otherwise, I will find myself incapable of taking care of myself and my loved ones.

Love yourself enough to leave enough of you for you!

*Therefore humble yourselves*
*under the mighty hand of God,*
*so that He may exalt you at the*
*proper time, having cast all your*
*anxiety on Him, because*
*He cares about you.*

(1 Peter 5:6–7)

# Today's Focus: Overwhelmed

## What does **overwhelmed** mean to you?

## How do you look and feel when you're **overwhelmed**?

# Today's Focus: Overwhelmed

List the top 3 tasks, people, or
responsibilities that **overwhelm** you.

What areas should be altered
or removed to create balance?

# Day 8

Today, I neglected to be still long enough to hear God's words concerning you. While this may sound insensitive or selfish, God simply described it as honest. Transparency during this process was much more important than the appearance of a perfect journal. That would only open the door for the spirit of pride.

On the other hand, **grace** is the free and unmerited favor of God. Therefore, He required me to label this as a Grace Page. For the sake of this journal, Grace Pages represent days when life interfered with my ability to seek God in order to receive His word to you. There are five Grace

Pages throughout this journal. Interestingly, in spiritual numerology, the number five represents grace.

*But He gives a greater grace.*
*Therefore, it says, "God is*
*opposed to the proud, but*
*gives grace to the humble."*

(James 4:6)

# Today's Focus: Grace

How would you describe **grace**?

How do you feel when someone extends **grace** to you?

# Today's Focus: Grace

Do you consider yourself to be **gracious**?

How does the **grace** page make you see your journey?

# Day 9

The ability to **discern** is defined by Google as the ability to perceive or recognize something. However, Strong's biblical dictionary defines it as the ability to distinguish. Thankfully, I realized today that my preparation for you requires a level of discernment. More importantly, it requires a level of transparency.

As I examine the challenges that I continue to face each day, I understand that there is a way that I have to respond to the enemy's tactics. You see, whenever I prepare to speak to a group of women, the enemy heightens the attack against me. That's how important you are to God. If I can be distracted from the assignment before me, then

I'll become incapable of discerning your needs before I reach you. (Sound familiar in your life?)

Similarly, when I ignore the spirits that are active around me, I begin to deceive myself. Naturally, it's easier to ignore what we have clearly discerned, in order to avoid confrontation and/or discomfort. So today I decided to inform the spirits of deception and depression that I would not entertain them.

Every day, I'm learning new strategies that prevent me from engaging with unwelcome spirits. Practically speaking, when I discern an unwanted spirit, I look it in the eye and let it know that I see it! I make a conscious choice not to converse with it. Then I can pray, using God's word, to stand against the spirit that is active.

As He continues to sharpen my discernment, I trust that it will strengthen my testimony and prayers on your behalf.

*And this I pray, that your love may overflow still more and more in real knowledge and all discernment, so that you may discover the things that are excellent, that you may be sincere and blameless for the day of Christ.*

(Philippians 1:9–10)

# Today's Focus: Discernment

Create your definition of **discernment**.

How do you know when you've **discerned** something?
(Example: Thoughts? Feelings?)

# Today's Focus: Discernment

Normally, do you follow what you've **discerned**?

How can you use **discernment** along your journey?

# Day 10

I would love to give a plausible reason for not disciplining myself for today's writing assignment. However, an excuse would nullify the fact that human nature caused me to become distracted. Thankfully, my distractions will not prevent God from reaching you as He promised! Hallelujah!

**Grace** is the free and unmerited favor of God. Therefore, He required me to label this as a Grace Page. For the sake of this journal, Grace Pages represent days when life interfered with my ability to seek God in order to receive His words for you. There are five Grace Pages throughout this journal. Interestingly, in spiritual numerology, the number five represents grace.

*For sin shall not be master over*
*you, for you are not under the*
*Law, but under grace.*

(Romans 6:14)

# Today's Focus: Grace

What are your thoughts about
**grace** since day 8 of this journal?

Have you extended **grace** to someone since day 8?
If so, how did it make you feel?

# Today's Focus: Grace

Have you made a recent mistake that
allowed someone to extend **grace** to you?

What did this **grace** page say to you?

# Day 11

T oday was the day that I saw what God said. He told me to go before the director of a local boys' school and ask him for permission to use his school as a venue for You Are the Storm. The meeting was arranged by a dear friend who clearly understood **God's plan** for you. When I arrived at the school, I was invited to the students' morning assembly. I found myself engulfed in worship with a gymnasium full of young men. Wow!

After an amazing experience, I began the scheduled meeting with the assistant director. I've never seen the hand of God move so clearly during a business meeting. He confirmed His instructions throughout the conversation. Then I learned that

the assistant director was a fellow speech thera-
pist who happened to love Jesus! She mentioned a
statement about believing, so I shared the foundation scripture for this event—Luke 1:45.

*And blessed is she who believed*
*that there would be a fulfillment*
*of what had been spoken to*
*her by the Lord.*

When the school's director joined the meeting,
his testimony confirmed God's choice. God didn't
need me to search the city for a location that would
allow me to speak to you. He had predetermined
a place where His presence was already welcome!

The director said yes!

*A person's gift makes room*
*for him and brings him*
*before great people.*

(Proverbs 18:16)

# Today's Focus: God's Plan

Create a **definition** for **God's plan**.

How do you know that something
is **God's plan** vs. Your plan?

# Today's Focus: God's Plan

List 1 or 2 things that you believe
are part of **God's plan** for your life?

What is the next step in following
**God's plan** for your life?

# Day 12

After an incredible meeting and confirmation, it would be easy to assume that I hastened to the feet of God for further instructions. However, I found myself fighting to resist every distraction that was sent my way. It's difficult to obey God, celebrate the victories, and ignore the schemes of the enemy. Clearly, the enemy didn't want me to reach you, so he used every possible tactic to prevent me from writing and going forth.

I thank God for extending grace AGAIN!

**Grace** is the free and unmerited favor of God. Therefore, He required me to label this as a Grace Page. For the sake of this journal, Grace Pages represent days when life interfered with my ability to seek God in order to receive His words for you. There are five Grace Pages throughout this journal. Interestingly, in spiritual numerology, the number five represents grace.

*And God is able to make all*
*grace overflow to you so that,*
*always having all sufficiency in*
*everything, you may have an*
*abundance for every good deed.*

(2 Corinthians 9:8)

# Today's Focus: Grace

What were your first thoughts when you
realized that this was a **grace page**?

Have your feelings changed
about giving yourself **grace**?

# Today's Focus: Grace

Do you give yourself enough **grace** to be imperfect?

What steps do you need to take
to help give yourself **grace**?

# Day 13

There is no way that I would ever have believed that I could end up with two consecutive days of empty pages in a journal that God instructed me to write! However, I am confident that He wants us to learn to embrace our imperfections in order to help others. Instruction from God required me to be vulnerable in every sense.

This is the epitome of being vulnerable! Challenges, pain, and frustration were growing, but I had to remain committed to His instruction concerning you. While completing this journal was necessary, He wanted you to see that this is a finished work that was done by His grace!!

**Grace** is the free and unmerited favor of God. Therefore, He required me to label this as a Grace Page. For the sake of this journal, Grace Pages represent days when life interfered with my ability to seek God in order to receive His words for you. There are five Grace Pages throughout this journal. Interestingly, in spiritual numerology, the number five represents grace.

*And God is able to make all
grace overflow to you so that,
always having all sufficiency in
everything, you may have an
abundance for every good deed.*

(2 Corinthians 9:8)

# Today's Focus: Grace

Do you think people abuse **grace**?

How should you respond when you
feel that someone has abused your **graciousness**?

# Today's Focus: Grace

How has God been **gracious** to you lately?

How can you use his **grace** to shape yours?

# Day 14

(Sometimes God speaks through a poetic message.)

I am marveled by the mere fact
That you continue to give the enemy power
You've emerged from such a low place
That nothing should be able to agitate you in this hour

I've called you out of darkness
And into My marvelous light
I've created a new being through you
So that you're able to stand and not fight

Today you walked higher than before
You understood your rightful position
As you silenced yourself and learned to ignore

Keep moving in the spirit, precious daughter
So that I'm able to guide you and cover you all the same
Life will slowly become much easier
Because you are relying on the power in My name

Diligently seek Me every day
And prepare yourself for a magnanimous shift
Your life is undergoing a transformation
And there is newness that will follow your speaking **gift**

*...for the gifts, and the calling of*
*God are irrevocable.*

(Romans 11:29)

# Today's Focus: Gift

Define **gift.**

How did it feel to discover the **gift** inside of you?

# Today's Focus: Gift

How do you use the **gift** inside of you?

What did this poetic message say to you?
(What action(s) do you need to take?)

# Day 15

oneliness is a word that is misunderstood by many. You see, when I say that I frequently find myself in a lonely space, it means that it's difficult to explain my journey to others. Sometimes I have to remain quiet, avoid gathe rings, minimize my conversations, and dedicate more time to prayer and worship. When I am attempting to hear exactly what God intends for me to do, it requires some degree of isolation.

In my world, loneliness does not refer to a life that is void of family, friendships, socialization, and/or other unique interactions. Those relation-ships offer support, encouragement, and love. They remind me that I am not ALONE!

Loneliness specifically relates to the nature of my walk with God. He doesn't have group meetings when He's giving me instructions, lol. So it is crucial that I begin to understand that natural loneliness is the breeding ground for spiritual intimacy with God. I had to long for Him more than I craved human contact. That became very difficult at times! (Hey, I am human, you know!)

My dear sister, one of the most powerful ways to battle moments and seasons of loneliness is to worship God! It's the place where you can find His consistent, powerful, comforting, calming, and loving presence! Allow Him to become your everything.

*You will make known to me the*
*way of life; in Your presence is*
*fullness of joy; in Your right*
*hand there are pleasures forever.*

(Psalms 16:11)

# Today's Focus: Loneliness

Which description of **loneliness** best describes you?

A.  The absence of people

B.  A place with God where you're frequently alone

Explain why.

According to your definition of **loneliness**,
is your experience desirable or undesirable?
Explain your response.

# Today's Focus: Loneliness

How do you move past **loneliness**?

Use today's message and your comments
to create 3 ways to respond to **loneliness**?

# Day 16

As the days grow closer to meeting you face-to-face, the intensity increases. While I wear a face that says, "I'm fine," my mind races, and I'm trembling with fear. Today will be a demanding day because I need to complete one season of my life in order to step into the next. The irony is that they are both occurring on the same day. God is showing me that He is in control.

For example, He gave specific instructions for my outfits to be worn during an upcoming photo shoot. When I arrived at the studio, one room's decor was a direct complement to the clothing that I was supposed to wear. Then my cousin showed me, in the studio, there were candles labeled with the word *storm*.

There can't be much more confirmation than that!

Sister, when God has called you to a particular place or a specific assignment, He sends reminders to encourage you. Those reminders help you to understand that you are on the right path.

You've been **chosen**, and I can't wait to see your face when you realize it!

> *But you are a chosen people, a*
> *royal priesthood, a holy nation,*
> *a people for God's own posses-*
> *sion, so that you may proclaim*
> *the excellencies of Him who has*
> *called you out of darkness into*
> *His marvelous light.*

(1 Peter 2:9)

# Today's Focus: Chosen

Describe **chosen**.

Describe how you feel when you're **chosen** to complete a task or join someone in what they're doing.

# Today's Focus: Chosen

What do you believe God has **chosen** you to do?

Using today's message, write
3 steps that you need to take.

# Day 17

As I am preparing to speak to you, I still have to try to maintain some measure of balance. However, I have to admit that it is definitely a weakness of mine. Wearing multiple hats requires me to allocate appropriate amounts of time for each role. Sometimes it feels impossible!

I'm preparing to speak on social media in order to redefine how I've presented myself. I've always wanted to maintain a professional image, but in this season, my professionalism isn't a badge of honor. The honor is serving God in truth and integrity. When I say (and do) what I've been instructed to say and do, He gets the glory! That's the purpose of my life.

In spite of the glitches with social media, I believe that God was glorified tonight. **Perfectionism** is not from God because it doesn't give Him room to refine us.

> *Indeed, there is not a righteous*
> *person on earth who always does*
> *good and does not ever sin.*

(Ecclesiastes 7:20)

# Today's Focus: Perfectionism

Describe **perfectionism**.

How do you feel when you are trying to be **perfect**?

# Today's Focus: Perfectionism

When do you find yourself trying to be **perfect**?

List 2 or 3 areas in which you need
to allow yourself to make mistakes?

# Day 18

Each day, there are little reminders that encourage me to continue to prepare for our introduction. So today I met with my team to discuss the specifics related to our special event. As I shared the details of God's plan, one of the members announced that she had a surprise! She had purchased a wig for my costume.

I immediately thanked her and referred to my cousin (another team member) because we had recently discussed the challenges with selecting a wig. The wig that I had purchased arrived in the wrong color. So this surprise gift was both kind and timely!

Another team member interjected that her company would purchase tickets for women who could not afford to buy one. Again, I referred to another team member with whom I had discussed the same subject. Multiple tickets were donated for *You Are the Storm*.

Sister, when God ordains a specific task, He makes **provision**!

*And my God will supply all your*
*needs according to His riches in*
*glory in Christ Jesus.*

(Philippians 4:19)

# Today's Focus: Provision

## Describe **provision**.

## What feelings do you experience when you don't have what you need?

# Today's Focus: Provision

Describe a recent time when
God made **provision** for you.

What steps can you take to show
God that you trust Him to **provide**?

# Day 19

The evidence says guilty
Though my heart doesn't want to say true
Everything points in the same direction
All the cards are stacked against you

When we believe what we desire
More than what we know is real
It means we are in denial
And we need more time to heal

Protecting yourself without honesty
Is a lie in and of itself
It robs you of practical thinking
And places your deliverance on an unreachable shelf

Try harder, precious sisters and daughters
To keep **truth** around your waist
Pass by everything that robs you of honesty
Flee the devil with extreme haste

*Stand firm, therefore, having*
*belted your waist with truth, and*
*having put on the breastplate of*
*righteousness.*

(Ephesians 6:14)

# Today's Focus: Truth

## Describe **truth**.

## How do you feel when you're not being **truthful**?

# Today's Focus: Truth

Describe a time when it was difficult to remain **truthful** about yourself or a situation.

What does the poetic message say to you? What action(s) do you need to take?

# Day 20

Google's definition of **abandon** is "to cease to support or look after (someone), to desert." Issues involving abandonment permeate my life across numerous settings. While I don't mind being home alone, when I experience significant time periods in which I am left alone, it feels as if I've been abandoned.

The root of my abandonment issue is deeply connected to instances in which I was left alone without answers, direction, or security. There have been so many times when I couldn't tell anyone how alone I felt. When there's an expectation that people will walk alongside you, encourage you, and support you as you grow, that's what you tend to expect! However, when disappointment and/or abandonment occurs, there is a void that is difficult to fill.

But God never leaves us!

> *...for He Himself has said, I will*
> *never desert you, nor will I ever*
> *abandon you...*

(Hebrews 13:5)

# Today's Focus: Abandonment

## Describe **abandonment**.

## Describe any feelings that connect you to **abandonment**.

# Today's Focus: Abandonment

Describe any experience with **abandonment**.

What action can you take to move past feelings of **abandonment**?

# Day 21

Even though you find yourself paralyzed
By a **pain** that you cannot explain
I'm asking you, precious daughter
To understand where you must remain

Remain nestled underneath the sound of My voice
Where the enemy cannot infiltrate your precious mind
Remain consistent in the study of My word
So that he's unable to rob you blind

Though he will attempt to steal, kill, and destroy
Remember that you have life more abundantly
Remember that Jesus is your portion
And He came that you might be free

Pain attempts to paralyze your very being
So that you're incapable of moving forward
I'm producing enough oil in you, daughter
To cause you to pray, fast, preach, and move onward

This is the season that I've called you to women
Although your personal pain wants to render you inept
I've given your pain a specific purpose
As it permeates anything superficial
with the intent to create depth

*Blessed be the God and Father of*
*our Lord Jesus Christ, the Father*
*of mercies and God of all*
*comfort, who comforts us in*
*all our affliction so that we*
*will be able to comfort those*
*who are in any affliction with*
*the comfort with which we our-*
*selves are comforted by God.*

(2 Corinthians 1:3–4)

# Today's Focus: Pain

## How would you describe **pain**?

## What does your emotional/mental **pain** feel like?

# Today's Focus: Pain

Are you currently experiencing
**pain** that is paralyzing you?

What does this poetic message say to you?
What action(s) do you need to take?

# Day 22

While this is the final Grace Page within this body of work, I continue to struggle to obey ALL of God's instructions. This journey involved numerous twists and turns that were sent to discourage me from completing this assignment. I knew that I had to finish, so God kept reassuring me that I wouldn't do anything without His grace. I had to BELIEVE that God was going to allow this event to manifest because He designed it. There was so much to be done in such a small amount of time, but it HAD to be done.

I'm thankful for the opportunity to confess that these Grace Pages represent an authentic walk with God, one that allows me to make mistakes while being obedient.

Embrace the grace of God as you grow!

**Grace** is the free and unmerited favor of God. Therefore, He required me to label this as a Grace Page. For the sake of this journal, Grace Pages represent days when life interfered with my ability to seek God in order to receive His words for you. There are five Grace Pages throughout this journal. Interestingly, in spiritual numerology, the number five represents grace.

*And He said to me, "My grace*
*is sufficient for you, for power*
*is perfected in weakness." Most*
*gladly, therefore, I will rather*
*boast about my weaknesses, so*
*that the power of Christ may*
*dwell in me.*

(2 Corinthians 12:9)

# Today's Focus: Grace

What thoughts enter your mind
when you hear the word **grace**?

Have your feelings changed from
the first **grace page** to the last?

# Today's Focus: Grace

Describe your most recent experience with **grace**.

Share the positive and/or negative
impact of the **grace pages.**

# Day 23

There is so much pain and confusion
That literally leaves you in despair
You don't have time for indiscretions
Or interactions with people who don't care

You have to move with a quickness
And a focus that cannot be shaken
You have to obey My commands
Because you won't be abandoned, nor forsaken

You're at the edge of something beautiful
Something never seen in this time
You will deliver a message
Specifically **designed** for those who are Mine

*"For I know the plans that
I have for you," declares the
Lord, "plans for prosperity
and not for disaster, to give
you a future and a hope."*

(Jeremiah 29:11)

# Today's Focus: Designed

Define **designed**.

How does it feel to know that
something was **designed** for you?

# Today's Focus: Designed

So far, which part of this journal was **designed** for you?

What does this poetic message say to you?
What action(s) do you need to take?

# Day 24

Stop clinging to folks for survival
Stop believing everything that they say
Stop leaning to media for instruction
Start bending your knees to pray

Stop looking for life's fulfillment
Within the arms of the young and old
Start looking to Me for restoration
Start standing and being more bold

Stop calling on people who betrayed you
Start looking to the hills for your strength
Start maximizing the power of your potential
Start optimizing your width, height, and length

You are more than a **conqueror,** sweet daughter
You were designed with incredible power
So live your life without any limitations
For I've called you to come forward in this hour

*But in all these things we*
*overwhelmingly conquer*
*through Him who loved us.*

(Romans 8:37)

# Today's Focus: Conqueror

## Define **conqueror.**

## How do you feel after you've **conquered** something?

# Today's Focus: Conqueror

Describe something that you need
to **conquer** in your life today.

What did the poetic message say to you?
What action(s) do you need to take?

# Day 25

Her skin is too dark
For the light in your eye
You hear her voice
But you don't recognize the prize

See her far beyond the attention from this week
You're making her ashamed
She can't stand because she's too weak

Yet, the **warrior** in this woman
Will be uncovered in just a while
It will be too late then, oh brother
Because her storm will reach for miles

She'll blow away uncertainty
She'll freeze the insecurities
She'll rain on unclean exchanges
She'll send hurricanes to all obscurities

*I will give thanks to You,*
*because I am awesomely*
*and wonderfully made…*

(Psalms 139:14)

# Today's Focus: Warrior

## Define **warrior.**

## How does it feel when you're **warring** for something?

# Today's Focus: Warrior

What kind of **warfare** are you experiencing today?

What did this poetic message say to you?
What action(s) do you need to take?

# Day 26

Indecisiveness has been a key player along this journey. My inability to make clear and definitive decisions has negatively impacted my life and the lives of those to whom I am connected. Unfortunately, much of my judgment has been clouded by emotions. However, emotions should never be the deciding factor for life-altering decisions.

My dependence upon the Holy Spirit has also been swayed by the power of my emotional and mental condition. During this time of preparation, I've asked God to help me so that I don't find myself walking aimlessly.

Remember to consider the guidance of the Holy Spirit in every decision. The opinions, responses, and suggestions of others may sometimes interfere with God's direction. He never misleads His children.

The key to my journey with Him has been, and will always be, remaining in our secret place.

*One who dwells in the shelter of*
*the Most High will lodge in the*
*shadow of the Almighty.*

(Psalms 91:1)

# Today's Focus: Indecisiveness

Describe **indecisiveness.**

What happens internally when you're **indecisive?**

# Today's Focus: Indecisiveness

Are there decisions that you haven't made because you're **indecisive?**

What steps can you take to make a **decision?**

# Day 27

There are very few days remaining
Before my encounter with you
There are only moments remaining
Before God does what He promised to do

So I'm praying for you, my dear sister
That your spirit is **preparing** even now
God is raising up a new generation
Of those who are preparing to move in His power

Don't be discouraged as you move into this new season
Don't be frightened by the things that you see
Be enlightened by the power of our Master
And the plans that He has for you and me

Keep pushing into this new year of promise
That will be exactly what our Father has said
It will be an encounter that you will remember
A time when you will be encouraged and spiritually fed

*For we are His workmanship,
created in Christ Jesus for good
works, which God prepared
beforehand so that we would
walk in them.*

(Ephesians 2:10)

# Today's Focus: Preparation

Define **preparation**.

How do you feel when you're **prepared** to do something?

# Today's Focus: Preparation

What are you **preparing** for in this season of your life?

What did this poetic message say to you?
What action(s) do you need to take?

# Day 28

Don't live in anguish, precious daughter
For I am your God, and I love you best
Some things appear to be unbearable
But I continue to call you blessed

Please begin to embrace your **journey**
As if you know that there is purpose for you
Your life carries significant value
There is something that I've called you to do

Please listen when I whisper instructions
Don't ignore Me when you see what I've said
Sometimes I operate through people
Other times I speak through what you've read

Continue to move forward in this hour
When this world seems to be in despair
I've planted your feet, My dear daughter
There's a reason that I've placed you there

Draw closer in the morning when I wake you
Listen longer after you've spoken your prayer
No one understands the design for you
No one can tell you how to prepare

I'll walk with you through trials and tribulations
I'll carry you through pain and devastation
I'll strengthen you when you feel incapable
I'll comfort your sorrows without hesitation

Then you will arise with great power
You'll stand victoriously before each of your foes
You'll reconcile unnecessary differences
And mediate when no one understands or knows

*Trust in the Lord with all your
heart, and do not lean on your
own understanding. In all your
ways acknowledge Him, and He
will make your paths straight.*

(Proverbs 3:5–6)

# Today's Focus: Journey

Define **journey**.

From the poetic message, select one
phrase that speaks to you and explain why.

# Today's Focus: Journey

## Where are you in your personal **journey**?

## What steps are you preparing to take?

# Day 29

I have given you **life**
And it, more abundantly
I have given you peace
And a time to break free

There is no weapon formed against you
That shall prosper, My child
You've suffered and cried
For just a little while

Now I'm giving you the keys
To open every door of provision
I've anchored you forever
Watch My words and My next decision

*The thief comes only to steal*
*and kill and destroy; I came so*
*that they would have life, and*
*have it abundantly.*

(John 10:10)

# Today's Focus: Life

Define **life**.

What are your feelings about your **life** today?

# Today's Focus: Life

What are you doing to enjoy this **life**?

What did this poetic message say about your **life**?

# Day 30

In over a decade of writing, God never repeats what He says to me. If I fail to write it down as He says it, the information is lost. Today, He extended an extreme amount of grace as He ended this journal by repeating these words:

"BE CELIBATE IN THE SPIRIT!"

*...because it is written: "You shall be holy, for I am holy."*

(I Peter 1:16)

# Today's Focus: Holy

## Define **holy**?

## How do the words **holy** and **celibate** make you feel?

# Today's Focus: Holy

"BE CELIBATE IN THE SPIRIT!"
What does this mean to you?

What will you take away from this journal?

# About the Author

S tephanie Parham is a native Clevelander who is a product of both the Cleveland and East Cleveland school systems. After graduating from Shaw High School, she attended Hampton University, where she earned a bachelor of arts degree in communication disorders. She returned to Ohio to complete her master's degree in speech-language pathology at Kent State University. Stephanie is the mother of an eighteen-year-old son, Justin, whom she refers to as her inspiration and gift. She has been married to her childhood friend, Shawn, for the past six years.

Stephanie has spoken for such groups as Alcoholics Anonymous, Narcotics Anonymous, Claudette's Kids Foundation, as well as church organizations in Ohio, Georgia, New York, and Florida. In 2016, she was featured twice on *Triumphant Praise* on KRGN 98.5 FM in Killeen, Texas, with Roland Stewart. Locally, she was interviewed in 2017 by Grace Roberts from 107.3 The Wave in Cleveland, Ohio. In 2022, she was interviewed by Cleveland's Jay the Gospel Kid on WOVU 95.9 FM.

Professionally, Stephanie worked as a speech-language pathologist for twenty-eight years until June of 2022. She retired to pursue entrepreneurship through her own company, Creative Communicative Connections, LLC.

Along her spiritual and professional journey, Stephanie is most thankful for her relationship with God. He has given her purpose beyond her pain as she speaks to encourage women through the power of her life-changing testimony.

# CREATIVE COMMUNICATIVE CONNECTIONS

reative Communicative Connections, LLC was created in May of 2020 after years of developing literature, training materials, and dramatic presentations. In July of 2020, CCC launched its first training in response to a public-speaking request for a group of psychology students at Cleveland State University.

In 2022, CCC created a virtual-speaker series that provided workshops in the following areas:

- Learning opportunities for children
- Marriage
- Financial literacy
- Personal development
- Childhood entrepreneurship
- Children's social-emotional health

# Let's Connect

Find more about Stephanie R. Parham at the following links!

Official Website: www.Stephanieparham.com

LinkedIn: Stephanie-parham-a84899208

Instagram: uback2u

Facebook: uback2u